REBEL GIRLS

Little Library

10 Women who Invent

Good Night Stories for Rebel Girls and all other Rebel Girls titles are available for bulk purchase for sale promotions, premiums, fundraising, and educational needs. For details, write to sales@rebelgirls.com.

This is a work of creative nonfiction. It is a collection of heartwarming and thought-provoking stories inspired by the lives and adventures of influential women. It is not an encyclopedic account of the events and accomplishments of their lives.

www.rebelgirls.com

Rebel Girls, Inc.
421 Elm Ave.
Larkspur, CA 94939

Text by Dinah Dunn
Art direction by Giulia Flamini
Graphic design by Kristen Brittain
Graphic design and additional illustrations: Alessandro Raimondo
Portrait illustrations: 4: Elisabetta Stoinich, 8: Izzy Evans,
12: Amy Phelps, 16: Irene Rinaldi, 20: Cristina Spano,
24: Naomi Anderson-Subryan, 28: Avani Dwivedi,
32: Thaiz Zafalon, 36: Fanesha Fabre, 40: Ren Capacio

Printed in China, 2023
10 9 8 7 6 5 4 3 2 1
ISBN: 979-8-88964-080-6

FSC
www.fsc.org
MIX
Paper | Supporting responsible forestry
FSC™ C018179

CONTENTS

Ada Lovelace

Mathematician

December 10, 1815–November 27, 1852 | UK

Once upon a time, there was a girl named Ada who loved to learn. At the time, most girls weren't taught math. But Ada's mother enjoyed it and taught it to her daughter. Ada picked it up quickly.

The 12-year-old also loved the idea of flying. So she studied birds to figure out how big their wings needed to be for their size. *Maybe if I could work it out, I could fly*, she thought. Ada never managed to soar like a bird. But she created a beautiful book full of drawings called *Flyology*.

When she was 17, Ada went to a ball. There, she met a grumpy old mathematician named Charles Babbage. They both loved math and soon became good friends.

Charles invited Ada to see a machine he had invented. He called it the Difference Engine. When it was finished, it would be able to add and subtract numbers. No one had ever done that before. Ada was hooked.

Charles had an idea for an even better machine that could do more than just add and subtract. Ada and Charles wrote letters back and forth, working out the details. Their machine would be huge! To run it, they'd need a huge steam engine.

Ada dreamed even bigger. *What if this machine could play music and show letters as well as numbers?* she wondered. She was describing a computer before computers were invented! Charles helped her write out ideas about what it could do. Her ideas were ahead of their time. Ada is sometimes called the first computer programmer.

SCAN TO HEAR MORE!

Inventor and Entrepreneur

Born November 26, 2008 | USA

Seven-year-old Cassidy wanted to enter a science fair. She was trying to think up a good idea. She found one in a funny place: her baby sister, Emily.

Cassidy noticed her mom was worried when Emily started to feed herself. It was important for Emily to learn to use a spoon on her own. But what if she cut her gums on the plastic? What if she hurt her throat? *There must be a way to design a better baby spoon*, Cassidy thought. And it was up to her to invent it.

Cassidy got right to work and came up with the Baby Toon! Made from a soft material, this spoon was easy for babies to hold. Even better—it was in the shape of a cute elephant.

The trunk of the elephant could hold only a tiny amount of food. That made it hard for babies to choke. And the square shape prevented babies from poking their throats.

When Cassidy presented her Baby Toon at the science fair, everyone agreed that her idea had a future. After years of working on her design, Cassidy took her invention to a TV show for people who want to start businesses.

The 12-year-old and her mom presented the Baby Toon with big smiles and even a little dance. The judges were impressed. Cassidy was happy when one of them agreed to put money toward making thousands of spoons.

By the time Baby Toon became a real company, Cassidy's little sister was old enough to eat with regular spoons. But that didn't matter. Emily was proud of the spoon her big sister had invented for her.

Gitanjali Rao

Scientist and Inventor

Born November 19, 2005 | USA

As a kid, Gitanjali was always full of ideas. When she learned that people in Flint, Michigan, didn't have clean drinking water, Gitanjali thought she could help. She began to work on an invention. It would find pollution in water and send the information to people's phones.

Gitanjali entered a competition where young scientists could come up with ways to fix real-world problems. Gitanjali was chosen to be paired with a scientist to make her idea real. She went to a lab filled with beakers, chemicals, and smart people in white coats. It was exciting!

With the help of the scientist, she was able to create her invention: Tethys, which was named after the

Greek goddess of fresh water. It's a fast way for people to test for pollution in their water. Her invention earned Gitanjali the title of America's Top Young Scientist.

The girl with the big ideas was just getting started! Gitanjali's next invention was a computer program called Kindly. It helped stop kids from getting bullied on the internet. It was so good that it was soon being used all over the world.

Once she was asked what advice she would give to young inventors. Gitanjali replied, "Dive in!" She knows every invention starts with an idea. But no idea is perfect. To make a great invention, you need to make a lot of mistakes. “Failure is the first step in learning, so develop your ideas without fear,” Gitanjali said.

In 2020, *TIME* magazine made Gitanjali their first-ever *TIME* Kid of the Year. Not only were her inventions cool, but they also made the world a better place. As Gitanjali likes to put it, “inventing” is just another word for “using science for kindness.”

SCAN TO HEAR MORE!

Jennifer Doudna

Biochemist and Entrepreneur

Born February 19, 1964 | USA

Not long ago, the loud ring of the phone pulled Jennifer out of a deep sleep.

"Hello?" she said, rubbing her eyes. A reporter was on the line. She asked what Jennifer thought about the Nobel Prize. It is the biggest award a scientist can get!

"Whose Nobel Prize?" she asked.

"You don't know?" the reporter laughed. "You won the Nobel Prize in Chemistry!"

While the award was a surprise, it came from a lifetime of loving chemistry. Jennifer grew up playing in the forests of Hawaii. There she became interested in plants and animals. *What makes them grow the way they do?* she wondered.

When she grew up, she began studying the chemistry of living things. In college, she got to work in a lab. She thought, *Wow! This is exactly what I want to be doing.*

One night, Jennifer met the scientist Emmanuelle Charpentier. They started talking about proteins and bacteria. These conversations led them to their invention, called CRISPR. CRISPR is like a tiny pair of scissors that can be used inside a person's body. The tool can cut out or change genes that cause diseases such as cancer.

After inventing it, Jennifer and Emmanuelle had many questions. What diseases could CRISPR cut? Are there other good reasons to cut genes? Are there dangers? To find the answers, Jennifer would need help from a huge team of scientists. She'd also need to build new tools.

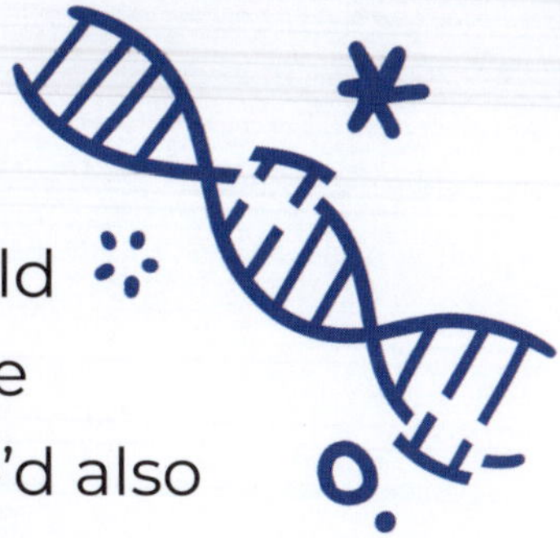

Jennifer and Emmanuelle started five different companies to figure out what CRISPR could do. They keep searching for answers, but CRISPR is already beginning to save lives.

Jennifer followed her passion. "Go for it," she tells other young scientists. "If you have a good idea, it's probably going to work out in some way." Who knows? You too may win a Nobel Prize.

Madam C. J. Walker

Inventor and Entrepreneur

December 23, 1867–May 25, 1919 | USA

As a young woman, Sarah Breedlove worked long hours, washing clothes in St. Louis, Missouri. It was around 1890, and she earned just $1.50 a day. She also took care of her daughter, went to school, and sang in the church choir.

Then she started losing her hair. Sarah didn't know why it was happening. She tried different creams, but nothing helped. At the time, most beauty products were made for white people. They didn't work for Sarah, who was Black. She decided to make her own cream with different ingredients. Soon, her hair grew back full and healthy.

If it worked for me, I bet it will work for other women, she thought.

Sarah decided to sell it. But it needed a unique name. So she made up something special. She began going door to door selling "Madam C. J. Walker's Wonderful Hair Grower."

As Madam, Sarah also created what she called the Walker System. It combined oils, heated combs, and a style of brushing that helped hair grow. Black women loved it.

Madam traveled the country showing women the Walker System. It was so popular that she had to train other women to sell her products too. She told them, "Don't sit down and wait for opportunities to come . . . Get up and make them!"

At one point, her company had more than 3,000 people working there—mostly Black women! She also opened a beauty school and factory in Pittsburgh, Pennsylvania.

Madam C. J. Walker became the first self-made female millionaire in the United States. More importantly, she helped Black women feel beautiful and proud.

SCAN TO HEAR MORE!

Patricia Bath

Ophthalmologist and Inventor

November 4, 1942–May 30, 2019 | USA

Once there was a girl named Patricia who created an invention so the blind could see. It wasn't magic—it was science.

Her love of science began with a chemistry set she got as a kid. The stacks of books her mother took out of the library only made it stronger.

Where Patricia grew up in Harlem, not many people went to medical school. But Patricia believed in her goal. She studied all the time. And her mom cleaned people's houses to get the money to send her to college.

When Patricia went to medical school, she became interested in eyesight. She worked at a clinic, testing people's eyes. She noticed that Black people were more likely to be blind or have bad eyesight than white people.

Why is that? Patricia wondered. She created a study to find out. The answer was simple: Black people didn't know when they needed to see eye doctors.

She found a way to fix the problem. She trained people to go out into the community to teach others about eye care. They would also bring patients to see eye doctors. This idea saved a lot of people's sight.

Next, Patricia decided to find a safer way to remove cataracts. A cataract is a cloudy film that can grow over people's eyes and make their vision blurry. If a doctor doesn't help, cataracts can cause blindness.

Patricia was a Black woman, and doctors in the United States didn't take her seriously. They didn't want to help with her ideas. So she went to Europe. There, she created a device called the Laserphaco Probe. Her invention made eye surgery easier and less painful. It helped people who had been blind for years see again.

Patricia never let the doubts of others get in the way of her ideas. She said, "Remember that the limits of science are not the limits of imagination."

Riya Karumanchi

Inventor and Entrepreneur

Born circa 2003 | Canada

One day, Riya visited a friend's house. She heard a bump. Then she heard a small clang. Her friend's grandmother kept bumping into things! The grandmother did not see very well. She used a cane when she walked.

Tap, tap, tap. The white cane made a sound as it hit the floor. Sometimes, it hit a chair or a wall. When that happened, the grandmother knew not to walk there.

The cane was helpful. But Riya thought it could be even more helpful. Maybe she could design a new one!

The school science fair was coming up. Riya and a friend began to work together. They asked lots of big questions. How could a cane help people "see"? What if the cane "knew" which way to go?

They made a prototype. Prototypes are models of new products. Inventors use them to test new ideas. Riya added sensors to the cane. When the sensors find an object, the cane begins to shake.

Riya also made it so the cane could give its users directions! One buzz meant turn left. Two buzzes meant turn right.

Riya and her friend called their clever invention the SmartCane.

There were so many exciting ideas at the science fair. But the SmartCane won first prize!

Riya kept working on her invention. She wanted her cane to help as many people as possible.

She learned how to code. She studied all kinds of cool technology. Next, Riya learned about starting and running a business. She spread the word about the SmartCane.

Big companies thought her idea was great! They gave her money to help her make more SmartCanes. Reporters asked Riya, *What is it like to be a young inventor?*

It's a wonderful time to try out new ideas, she explained. *The worst that can happen is you learn.*

Solveiga Pakštaitė

Inventor and Entrepreneur

Born May 21, 1992 | Lithuania, Norway, and UK

Solveiga was a curious Lithuanian girl growing up in the United Kingdom. She had light-brown hair, bright-red glasses, and a mind that was always asking questions. *How can we take care of our planet?* she wondered. And, *What can we do to make sure everyone feels included?*

In college, Solveiga studied inclusive design. Inclusive designers make inventions that help people of all abilities live better. She studied how people who couldn't see traveled on buses and trains. She talked to lots of people and asked about their lives.

One question she asked was, *How do you know when your food is no longer good to eat?* Most people would read a date stamped on the food label. But people who had problems with their vision couldn't see the tiny letters.

When Solveiga thought about the question, she started to wonder how food companies came up with those dates anyway. The more she learned, the more she realized many of the dates were wrong. People were throwing away perfectly good food. In fact, 70 percent of the food thrown away in the UK is safe to eat. What a waste!

Solveiga decided to create a solution to this huge problem. She founded a company called Mimica. She hired scientists and engineers. Together they made a label that measures food's freshness. When the food is good, the label feels smooth. When the food goes bad, the label turns bumpy.

The awesome invention is already being used on drink caps. Solveiga hopes it will be on lots of food packages soon. Until then, she'll keep asking questions and making inventions.

Valerie Thomas

Astronomer and Inventor

Born February 8, 1943 | USA

One day, a young girl picked up a book called *The Boys' First Book of Radio and Electronics.* Valerie thought, *I'm not a boy. But who cares? This is really interesting!*

When her dad took apart their television to fix it, Valerie asked if she could help. *This is too hard for girls*, her father said. But Valerie wanted to find out how things worked.

In college, she studied math. Later, she got a top job at NASA. There she was working on something way more difficult than a television: the world's first satellite, *Landsat 1*. The satellite would circle the Earth in outer space and take pictures. Valerie was in charge of the part of the satellite that sent images back to Earth. These photos helped scientists learn about the weather.

In 1976, Valerie visited a science museum and saw something that would change her life. It was a light bulb, not connected to anything, still shining brightly. How did it do that? It looked so real!

The answer was a trick created by mirrors. They reflected the light from a hidden second light bulb to make it look as if the first bulb was on. *I wonder if I could do this with other images,* she thought.

That gave Valerie a great idea. She started studying what could be done with mirrors and light. Her invention was called the illusion transmitter. NASA uses it in its spaceships.

Valerie's invention is also used by doctors to look inside the human body. One day, it may also project 3D videos from your television right into your living room!

Valerie has come a long way from trying to fix televisions. But she still loves to figure out how things work.

Xóchitl Guadalupe Cruz López

Inventor

Born January 1, 2009 | Mexico

In Los Altos de Chiapas in the mountains of Mexico, there lived a little girl named Xóchitl. In her town, it was cold most of the year. People were often sick. Xóchitl was only seven years old, but she worried about her older neighbors.

She knew the cold baths people were taking weren't helping them when they were sick. But to heat up the water, people had to chop down trees for firewood. They couldn't afford any other kind of heater. *How can I make a heater without harming the forests?* Xóchitl thought. The answer that came to her was simple: use people's trash!

Xóchitl loved science. She was always coming up with cool ideas. So she took out paper and a pencil and spent weeks working on a design for a water heater.

Finally, her design was ready. She painted 10 recycled water bottles black to trap heat from the sun. Then she connected them with 50 feet of black hose. Her dad helped her install the project on the roof of their house. Now her family had hot water for their baths!

When it was all done, Xóchitl added up what she'd spent. Her heater had cost just $30 to build and it did exactly what it was supposed to do. It also reused trash that would otherwise pollute the planet.

People all over Mexico read about her project. They were amazed that a young girl had come up with such a useful invention. She even won an award that was given every year to outstanding women scientists. It had never been given to a kid before!

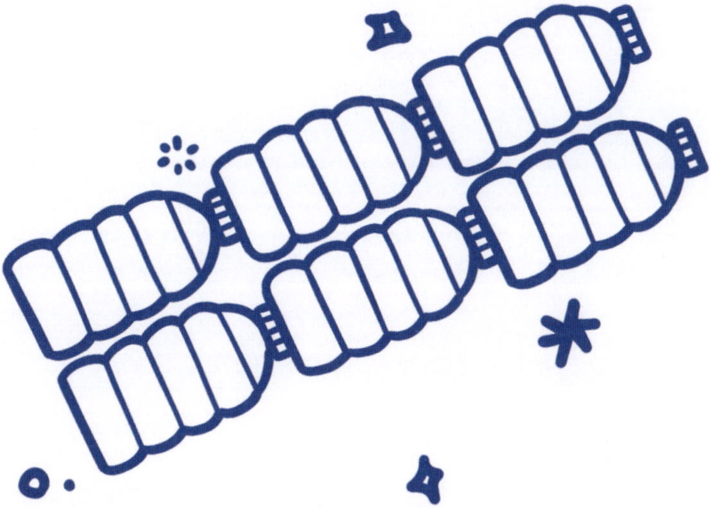

About Rebel Girls

Rebel Girls is a global, multi-platform empowerment brand dedicated to helping raise the most inspired and confident generation of girls through content, experiences, products, and community. Originating from an international best-selling children's book, Rebel Girls amplifies stories of real-life women throughout history, geography, and field of excellence. With a growing community of nearly 20 million self-identified Rebel Girls spanning more than 100 countries, the brand engages with Generation Alpha through its book series, award-winning podcast, events, and merchandise. With the 2021 launch of the Rebel Girls app, the company has created a flagship destination for girls to explore a wondrous world filled with inspiring true stories of extraordinary women.

As a B Corp, we're part of a global community of businesses that meet high standards of social and environmental impact.

Join the Rebel Girls community:

Facebook: facebook.com/rebelgirls
Instagram: @rebelgirls
Twitter: @rebelgirlsbook
TikTok: @rebelgirlsbook
Web: rebelgirls.com
Podcast: rebelgirls.com/podcast
App: rebelgirls.com/audio

If you liked this book, please take a moment to review it wherever you prefer!